D1474417

The Library of Intergenerational Learning

Native Americans

Apache Children and Elders Talk Together

E. Barrie Kavasch

The Rosen Publishing Group's
PowerKids Press™
New York

Our respect and gratitude to the Apache people, their amazing history, and bright future.

Published in 1999 by The Rosen Publishing Group, Inc.
29 East 21st Street, New York, NY 10010

Copyright © 1999 by The Rosen Publishing Group, Inc.

First Edition

Book Design: Danielle Primiceri

Photo Credits: Cover and all inside photos by JJ Foxx/NYC.

Kavasch, E. Barrie.
    Apache children and elders talk together/by E. Barrie Kavasch.
        p.   cm.—(Library of intergenerational learning. Native Americans)
    Summary: Explores the culture and traditions of the Apache people through the voices
    of Apache children and older people.
    ISBN 0-8239-5225-8
    1. Apache Indians—Juvenile literature. [1. Apache Indians. 2. Indians of North
    America—New Mexico.] I. Title. II. Series: Kavasch, E. Barrie. Library of intergenerational
    learning. Native Americans.
    E99.A6K38 1998
    973'.04972—dc21   97-49267
                                                                        CIP
                                                                        AC

Manufactured in the United States of America

Contents

I Am Apache

My name is Clay Geronimo. I live in Mescalero, New Mexico. I am nine years old, and am proud to be Apache. I am also proud to be a **descendant** (dee-SEN-dent) of Geronimo. Geronimo was a famous Apache leader who lived more than 100 years ago. He was a great fighter. He fought to protect Apache people. Geronimo was also a great Medicine Man.

Our family lives on Geronimo Loop near

Clay rides a horse just like his relative Geronimo did long ago.

4

the tribe's center on the **reservation** (reh-zer-VAY-shun). Our Mescalero Apache Reservation is near Sierra Blanca, or the White Mountains. The mountain is **sacred** (SAY-kred) to our people.

This summer I went to 4-H Steer School in Albuquerque for one week. I took Alfred, who is my new steer. I learned about taking care of big animals. I like feeding Alfred, who lives on my grandpa's farm. Taking care of Alfred is a lot of work! I also like to draw **rodeo** (ROH-dee-oh) pictures and make scrapbooks. I ride my horse. His name is Ernie. I especially like to ride Ernie in the Annual Mescalero **Celebration** (sel-uh-BRAY-shun) Parade on the Fourth of July.

Clay takes special care of his animals. He feeds them and gives them water every day. ▶

An Elder Speaks: Eva Geronimo

I'm Eva Geronimo, and I'm Clay's mother. Clay is a good artist. He also plays a guitar and a drum and loves to sing Western music. He and his cousins like Western and line dancing.

I'm glad Clay is in 4-H. Taking care of the animals is a lot of **responsibility** (ree-spon-sih-BIL-ih-tee). Clay learns a lot from this program. Not only am I Clay's mom, but I am also a granddaughter of Geronimo. We are proud to be his descendants. Geronimo is such a popular name that other people use it too.

I work with the Apache Elderly Program. Each month we take elderly, or older, people into the mountains to collect Indian medicines. We also gather **traditional** (tra-DISH-un-ul) Indian wild foods. The young people are starting to work in this program too. This way, they learn how to speak Apache from the older people. Clay often comes with me after school to the Elderly Program.

Eva Geronimo has made teaching the ways of the Apache a part of her life. ▶

Clans and Bands

My name is Robert Geronimo. I am Eva's older brother. My wife, Iris, and I live near Eva and Clay. We have five grown children and many grandchildren.

The Apache nation is made up of nine bands, or groups. Each band includes **clans** (KLANS) and other related families. The Mescalero Apache Reservation is home to the Mescalero, Chiricahuas, and Lipans. They all settled here in the early 1900s. Many of the Apache families live in houses along the Tularosa Canyon. Our bands are more important to us than our clans. There are also Jicarilla Apache, Western Apache, and Kiowa-Apache **tribes** (TRYBZ). Today, Apaches live in New Mexico, Arizona, and Oklahoma.

◀ *Robert Geronimo was a rodeo cowboy when he was young. He also helped to build many of the roads that run through the Mescalero Reservation.*

Celebrations

I'm Ellyn Bigrope. My family and grandchildren live nearby on the reservation. I enjoy talking with school groups and visitors about the Apache way of life. They ask me many questions. We **honor** (ON-er) our celebrations. Our big celebration is the Fourth of July Ceremonial. This is the Coming of Age **Ceremony** (SER-eh-mohn-ee) for our Apache maidens. It honors the time when a girl prepares to enter womanhood. Every piece of clothing in this ceremony has meaning. Special items bring special powers to the

Ellyn understands that it's important to teach others about Apache culture to keep it alive and strong.

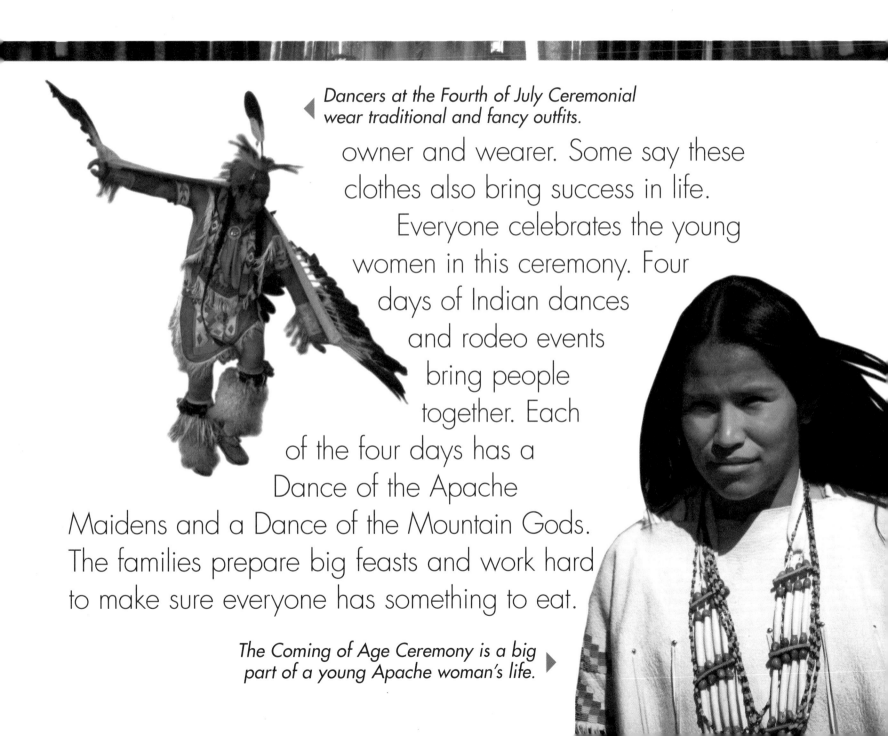

Dancers at the Fourth of July Ceremonial wear traditional and fancy outfits.

owner and wearer. Some say these clothes also bring success in life. Everyone celebrates the young women in this ceremony. Four days of Indian dances and rodeo events bring people together. Each of the four days has a Dance of the Apache Maidens and a Dance of the Mountain Gods. The families prepare big feasts and work hard to make sure everyone has something to eat.

The Coming of Age Ceremony is a big part of a young Apache woman's life. ▶

An Elder's Story

"I knew from the time I was small that I would follow my traditions," says Nathanial "Stan" Chee. Stan is an Apache Medicine Man. "I like to work with the native medicines and healing ways. This is what my father and grandfathers did. My mother and grandmothers also worked with native medicines. My Apache ways are strong. I always like healing people.

"As I guide one of the maidens through her Coming of Age Ceremony, I pray for her and for our people. That is part of the ceremony. Then I go with the men into the forest. I bless the trees before they cut them for our ceremonies. We chant for a long time as we ask the Great Spirits to bless the girls. The blessing songs continue as we work to raise the teepees that are a part of the ceremony. We also help each family build their cooking fire for the celebration."

◀ *Stan Chee enjoys teaching what he knows about healing to his grandsons.*

Our Lands

Kelly Pellman lives on the Mescalero reservation. "I am eleven years old, and I go to Mescalero School," Kelly says. "I like to ride my bike with my cousins and friends along the roads of the reservation." Kelly and her friends are excited about the big Fourth of July Parade and celebrations.

Lamar Victor is Kelly's cousin. He's twelve years old. He also likes to ride his bike with the kids on the reservation. "We are so lucky to live here in the mountains of southern New Mexico," says Lamar. "More than 3,000 Apache people live here. My family lives in a modern house and I go to school. We make **brush arbors** (BRUSH AR-berz) and pitch our teepees for our special ceremonies."

The beautiful mountains of southern New Mexico are home to Lamar, Kelly, and the Mescalero tribe. ▶

Families

My name is Meredith Begay. I am an Apache Medicine Woman. My husband, Keith, is Navajo. His grandfather was a Medicine Man. Our family is just full of leaders and healers! I often guide one of the Apache maidens through her ceremonial **duties** (DOO-teez). Our oak brush arbor shelters us from the hot sun and high winds of early July as we gather for this ceremony. Preparing for the ceremony brings us to our family camp on the ceremony grounds.

My work with the herbs and medicines of the people gives me peace. It is a big part of my life and family and who I am. It also helps to keep us all strong.

◄ *Meredith is an Apache Medicine Woman. She is respected far and wide as well as in the Apache tribe.*

The Dance of the Mountain Gods

The Dance of the Mountain Gods celebrates the miracles of living and healing. The dance started long ago. A **legend** (LEH-jend) tells how two boys were saved from death by the Mountain Gods. These gods showed the boys a special dance. Today, the Apaches perform the same dance to drive away sickness and problems from their lives. It also brings good health and happiness to those who see it. This traditional dance is repeated each night during the four days of the Coming of Age ceremony. They are an important part of Apache **culture** (KUL-cher).

The Dance of the Mountain Gods is performed at night by the Crown Dancers. It reminds the Apache people of the dance's beginnings. ▶

18

Food and Prayers

Each day before dawn, a special prayer is said. Prayers are also given at the beginning of special events. It is important to the Apaches that everyone is blessed. An elder starts the prayer with thankfulness to Usen, or God. A guest from another tribe may be asked to pray. Prayers keep the Apache strong and close to their traditions. They pray so they will always have enough food.

Delicious frybread is made for the dancers. Some people like to put chopped lettuce and tomato on top of their frybread. This is called an Indian Taco. Corn soup, potato salad, and chili are other favorite foods. On the last day of the festival, a few traditional wild foods are cooked. People like to try the wild spinach, yucca fruit, and wild beans. These are healthy foods from the earth. Apache **ancestors** (AN-ses-terz) once ate these foods too.

Traditional Apache foods are often served at ceremonial gatherings. Here the Apache are celebrating around the ceremonial teepee on the Fourth of July.

Futures

Wendell Chino is a respected Apache elder and has been president of the Mescalero tribe for many years. "We hope that we can hold onto the best of the old culture, which is the **wisdom** (WIZ-dum) and the beauty of the traditions of our ancestors," he says.

The hope of the Apache is for all children to have an education. Apache children have many talents and a lot of energy. Thanks to strong leaders and traditions, they have bright futures ahead of them.

Apache kids like Crystal Geronimo have a colorful history and an exciting future.

Glossary

ancestor (AN-ses-ter) A relative who lived before you.

brush arbor (BRUSH AR-ber) A shelter made of trees that protects against strong winds.

celebration (sel-uh-BRAY-shun) A special day or time of year in which the importance of something is honored.

ceremony (SER-eh-mohn-ee) An act or series of acts that are done on certain occasions.

clan (KLAN) People who are related within a tribe.

culture (KUL-cher) The beliefs, customs, and art of a group of people.

descendant (dee-SEN-dent) A relative of an ancestor from long ago.

duty (DOO-tee) A job; something that should be done.

honor (ON-er) To show admiration or respect for someone.

legend (LEH-jend) A story that comes from the past.

reservation (reh-zer-VAY-shun) An area of land set aside by the government for Native Americans to live on.

responsibility (ree-spon-sih-BIL-ih-tee) Something that a person must take care of and complete.

rodeo (ROH-dee-oh) A riding competition where people compete on horseback.

sacred (SAY-kred) Something that is highly respected and considered to be very important.

traditional (tra-DISH-un-ul) To do things the way a group of people has done them for a long time.

tribe (TRYB) A group of people united by the same ancestors.

wisdom (WIZ-dum) Knowledge and understanding.

Index

J970.1
Kasasch

Date Due
